The Café Writers Norfolk Commission

Strangers Hall is the product of the second Café Writers Norfolk Commission. The Commission is a new annual poetry competition open to recent graduates from a creative writing based course at Norwich School of Art and Design and the UEA. Patrons of the Commission, Kate and Dominic Christian are passionate about Norfolk and wanted to support emerging literary talent, and build a body of poetry which responds to the county in some way. They will generously donate £3,500 annually, for the lifetime of Commission, which provides prize money for the winner and funds the making of collections such as this.

The judges of the 2007 Café Writers Norfolk Commission were patron Kate Christian, Nathan Hamilton Director of Egg Box Publishing, Caroline Gilfillan former Chair of Poetry-next-the-Sea, and poet Esther Morgan. One of the things that we liked about Meirion Jordan's proposal was his intention to explore and respond to the role of outsiders in Norwich from its beginnings as a Saxon settlement in post-Roman Britain, through to the modern city as home to a substantial international student population.

Helen Ivory
Norwich, Spring 2009

For further information about the Commission and how to apply for it, please contact Helen Ivory.
helen.ivory@ntlworld.com

About the Author

Meirion Jordan was born in Wales and went to school in Swansea. He studied mathematics at Somerville College, Oxford, and took an MA in creative writing at UEA, Norwich. His work has appeared widely in poetry magazines from *Rialto* to the *TLS*, and his first collection of poems, *Moonrise*, is published by Seren. He has recently been awarded a bursary by the Welsh Academy towards the completion of a new work on the Arthurian Legend in Wales.

Strangers Hall

by

Meirion Jordan

Edited by Helen Ivory

GATEHOUSE PRESS LTD

Gatehouse Press Limited
Cargate Lane, Saxlingham Thorpe
Norfolk NR15 1TU
www.gatehousepress.com

First Published in Great Britain by
Gatehouse Press Limited 2009

ISBN 978-0-9562083-1-6

Cover design by Toni Hayden based on an early MS by kind
permission of The Bodleian Library

Printed and bound in Great Britain by
the MPG Books Group, Bodmin and King's Lynn

Contents

Preface *i*

The museum after hours (1) *1*
The foundations *2*
The layer of ash *3*
The undercroft *4*
The vestibule *5*
The parlour *6*
The anchorhold *7*
The oubliette *8*
The oriel window *9*
The kitchen *10*
The workshop *11*
The private chapel *12*
The library *13*
The great hall *14*

The magazine *15*
The garden *17*
The vestry *18*
The drawing room *19*
The stage door *20*
The fireplace *21*
The bedchamber *23*
The study *24*
The storm drain *25*
The auditorium *26*
The cockpit *27*
The garret *28*
The grand civic space *29*
The museum after hours (2) *30*

Notes on Strangers Hall *33*

Preface

This short collection of poems takes its title from the museum of the same name in Norwich city centre. Where possible I have tried to link their subjects in some way to the history of the building in which the museum is based, or the layout of the museum as it now stands, but this has not always been possible, nor has it always been in the interests of making these poems an enjoyable and varied selection from the histories of outsiders – a term which, like much else here of historical character, I have at times interpreted with some freedom – in Norwich. It is not a representative selection, nor is it intended as an overly lucid and revealing one: these poems are not a work of history, even though history figures largely in them. It is true, they fall in a loosely chronological sequence, but there is little matter here that will seem new to the student of these histories, unless they are interested in the verse itself. The events and circumstances of the past appear, but I have made no especial effort to explain them or their relation to one another, to form hypotheses which are substantiated by the facts of history.

This is, perhaps, as it should be. Exploring the past with a rational and searching eye is a skilled pursuit, not one to be entered into casually, and I make no apology for the fact that to obtain a comprehensive understanding of the contexts for some of these poems would present the reader with an intellectual challenge. But this is precisely the point: such a challenge is implicit in this work, and its absence would be telling; if these poems do not take it upon themselves to explain, they do attempt to make the past available, even tangible, in the way that all art strives to deliver experiences beyond itself.

Yet in the main, these poems are intended as a celebration of the histories they describe, of the rich traditions of Norman, Walloon, or Dutch immigrants, and of religious and political dissent that Norwich has hosted throughout the centuries. Some of this history is well attested in the historical records, as with much of the material pertaining to 18th- and 19th-century figures like Harriet and James Martineau, or the diarist Henry Crabb Robinson. More often than not there are a few tantalizing records and then silence, as with the disturbing murder of the boy who would become St. William of Norwich, or the brief and bloody visit of Sweyn Forkbeard in his fifteen-year campaign to become king of the English. In some places, as with the pillaging of Roman Caistor St. Edmunds (Venta Icenorum) for stone to build the earliest settlements at Norwich, there is nothing but a patchwork of archaeological evidence to indicate what took place. Sometimes there is not even that.

I will readily admit that at times I have had to work creatively with what records history has left, and lapse occasionally into what can only be described as historical fiction. Much of what the historian would wish to include has been left implicit out of deference to my audience, or is wholly absent. Where I have embellished the available facts, however, I have done so only in the sense of bridging the gaps in the records, of fleshing out the real with both the conjectures of historians and the drama that is native to this art: in short, I have done my best to avoid any serious distortion of the facts.

This may seem like a fairly obvious caveat, and indeed it is. Adopting such a position towards history is part of the responsibilities of the poet, just as it is their responsibility to attempt to engage with wider concerns than their own immediate circumstance. Such an effort is fraught with difficulties, of course, but to refuse to do so is often the most glaring sin of omission in the work of any poet. This may be only my understanding, but it nonetheless qualifies what I mean by this work as a celebration of certain histories: by bringing these aspects of the past to a new audience, I hope to encourage others to engage in their own understanding of the fabric of history; these poems, almost equal parts fact and fiction, are perched on the very cusp of history, and their aim is to draw others over the edge into the remarkable territories beyond.

Nevertheless, I have tried to make the book as closely tied to its sources as I can. Hence my decision to include notes on the context of the poems, and some images of interest or relevance along with them, to capture as much as is possible the endless sense of context that is the distinction of history. I hope that this is the case. I hope also that this book will contain something new, something both entertaining and rewarding for you, the reader, and I hope that this book is only the beginning and very smallest part of that reward.

The museum after hours (1)

the small sounds.
the shifting
of crockery, the faint cries

of a sleeper.
the pages
of a letter being turned.

step after step
the other rooms
grow louder

or further away:
moonlight throngs
the leads

the stars
sink nearer
or deeper into time;

and quiet presses
ears to the wall
when

in other rooms
the listeners
inhale the silence

as we tread.

The foundations

Caistor was town when Norwich was none;
Norwich was built with Caistor's stone
*   - Norfolk proverb*

let us begin with this, the handywork
of Giants, this stone, cadged or bartered,
cursed at, mounded up, re-sold,
mislaid, re-laid, demolished (twice)
set fire to, settled on and settled into,
dined on, laboured on, lived in and died in,
furnished, unfurnished, briefly entailed,
re-faced, defaced, re-bought, abandoned,
ruined, restored and mortgaged, missed:
the ashlar and flints, the mortar and bricks.

The layer of ash
(Sweyn Forkbeard sacks Norwich, 1004)

Sweyne is cyning:
as proclaimed
and coupons provided
Sweyn fleet-master
each of his warriors
raiders of shopping-malls

Sweyn Saxon-killer
on promotional tokens
by Coca-Cola;
far-feared sailor
a seasoned ravager;
pronounce him king.

By the public library
kneel to do homage:
they honour with tribute;
on billboards and posters
over the ephemeral
edges of his realm

bishops and layabouts
his is the name
Sweyn kingdom-taker
or between potsherds;
and crumbled earthenware
he asserts his rule.

He fades readily
into the clay-pits
busy with mud:
into cleft house-posts
where avuncular bin-men
'May the king live forever:'

his fork-beard receding
the clear estuary-ways
into the coins that made him;
among howe-grown cinquefoil
come bearing flattery:
Sweyn is king.

The undercroft

peat-smells, herring smack-smells,
the tallow reek and pitch,
caked dirt and woodsmoke
chicken-feed and pigs;

coarse ales and light ales,
rare ink and salt,
priest-hands and farm hands,
linen rags and paper;

stored urine, saltpetre,
tanning smells downriver;
wheat dust, grave dust,
a handful of pepper;

pork fat and incense,
bread and slops and bacon,
the wool smells, the silk smells,
the doctor and the reeve,

the day-smells and night-smells,
the snow and summer middens,
the split buds and crushed bark
and the deepening leaves.

The vestibule
(Herbert de Losinga, first bishop of Norwich)

Why do these masters, in their absence
keep me waiting like their villain?
Clearly I am a man of substance

yet I wait here as on penance
with nothing but the stones to sit on
thanks to these masters, in their absence.

You may see just from my garments -
silk from Tarsus, costly ermine -
that I am a man of substance

and my lands, in their abundance
almost eclipse my holy calling:
do these masters, in their absence

not recall the ghostly judgements
my reverend estate determines?
Or that such a man of substance

will not hang here, in a balance
to be weighed like wheat or herring!
Fie on these masters, in their absence
since I am such a man of substance.

The parlour

('Deus-adiuvet', Jew of Norwich, murdered 1146;
St. William of Norwich, murdered 1144)

Blood libel. Ritual. You have heard the talk,
the faces turned inwards from midnight shutters
that smile jauntily in the candlelight to say:
The Jew, The Jew. It is too late.

Already the boy is turning to a saint; and at the root
you knew, perhaps, the same things
drove them all: the smiling cook who drew the boy away,
the debtor knight whose men came after you

with knives as long as smiles. And him, the gagged one,
stabbed and sweetly putrefying in the wood,
which later, smelling money, priests would euphemise
"an odour of sanctity". Some measure of them all

it was, the perfect balance, the Byzantine weight,
the palm-grease of an Archdeacon's cook. You had
that measure, and in turn they sought you out.
Murdered yourself, yourself a prelude

to more murders, you within their talk became
the dark binary of the golden boy, forever circling
his luminance in that night of souls, the rumour
of an angel bearing up their world:

a golden one. Two-faced. Smiling and cold.

The anchorhold

*...me thought it might well be that I should
by the sufferance of god ... be tempted of fiendes
before I should die.*
                          - Julian of Norwich

Anchor me fast, my GOD:
desire me not this moment
to depart, nor draw up my soul
through that small window,
opening on heaven,
where this world enters in.

Let not my thoughts to wander
from this place, nor dwell
upon the muffled footsteps
of those soft, muttering people
or whoever it might be
that passes my cell:

nor let me spend
a further hour, a further minute
listening at these walls;
bring me disease or revelation,
some provocation to remove
my hand from this smooth skin,

the stone, which I have prayed
might be transfigured as
the flesh of CHRIST. These outer words
ripple, like echoes falling
in a well. I dread my wakefulness,
the slow passing of stars

and the cell's cold. LORD,
I pray for my temptation.
I press my cheek
against the wall, I press
against these outer worlds.
I wake. I pray. I sleep.

The oubliette

Bartholomew
truly wrongfully
and without reason
I am shut in this prison.

Truly wrongfully
I am taken:
and shut in this prison
far from you, or help,

I am taken
into the dark to sojourn
far from you, or help,
or sun, or season:

into the dark, to sojourn
until doom, or mercy,
sun, or season
look in upon me.

Held without doom, or mercy
and without reason;
God look upon me,
Bartholomew.

The oriel window

Glasse beyond the seas, and with no glass of England
- Covenant for windows of the Beauchamp Chapel

Let there be windows, full lights
of grisaille, and yards of it,
fine leading with no unseemly work
and with no glass of England.

Let there be saints, and ancient
armorial designs, pictures of donors
pierced by death's arrow or jumbled
among heavenly choirs,
let there be parables, and miracles,
and the one forbidden tree
with no glass of England.

Let there be goblets for rich suppers,
of green glass, and others clear
with cobalt blue touching their stems,
and let the light display ripples
in their bowls, as they fill
and with no glass of England.

Let there be Flemish wares
and Rhenish wares brought in
for the magnates' chambers;
let there be glittering cloths
among the very highest beams
with no glass of England.

Let there be halls, and colleges,
let there be manses and palaces
for the length of the shires and hundreds
with no glass of England;

Let there be sunlight, and firelight,
with torches in winter, with droplets
and bottles to fill with it, to run over
all the days of the anointed land
and with no glass of England.

9

The kitchen

it fades, it
is already gone:
the looming of figures
in woodsmoke, in steam,
the belching fireplace dragons
pensive,
withdrawn into bas-relief

      but sunlight
      weathering old tiles wrings
      a detritus of patterns,
      silhouettes tucked
      behind dust-motes combine
      to a man's shadow
      outlined in cracked clay

         it is like this
         sometimes,
         when all that can
         be found is the range
         throbbing with evening sunlight,
         the birds making Te Deum
         in the yard

            and the shadows
            through small limewashed spaces
            escaping, in their hundreds
            west, through the open hands
            of a window, a telephone wire,
            a tree.

The workshop
(Dutch artisans in Norwich, 16th and 17th centuries)

So much, then, for the weavers,
for the fingertips pricked bloodless
from turkey-work. After hours

the master comes to shutter
the darkened windows, snuff
the late candles:

where I see you still,
still bent at the weft, drawing-in
as night presses, while the moon

lurches from thread to thread
of your draw-loom sky.
I hear you passing the shuttle

through the darkened house,
through all the years of spindle
and distaff; becoming thin,

tugging in threads
like shadows. Sometimes
I wake to find your house

swirling in the breeze,
the boys and journeymen
stiffening into tapestry;

sometimes I rise, hearing
a nightingale trapped
in the cage of a warping mill

only to touch its wings
in a sky of silk, that are hands,
that are your very own.

The private chapel

(Thomas Sotherton, Sheriff and Mayor of Norwich;
Elizabeth Cooper, burnt for heresy, 1563)

Did she hear voices, then, Elizabeth
who stood in church, whom I had known,
and served with, crying I am
no listener for this popery to the crowd?
They say she did, that she spent nights
shouting in sleep, that her husband
beat her, that before she died she signed
a statement damning papists, Queen Mary
and myself. These rumours. What else
could I do? I am an officer of law
and when the law demands that I must
drag a pewterer's wife to jail, hear out
her meagre trial and lastly lead her down
towards the Lollards' pit, there to await
the flame – what else could I do?
They know, the market fishwives,
pedlars, beggars, tanners, thieves,
and they come whispering round my eaves
and I am only lucky that I am too old to hear.
I watched her falter and affirm
her faith to the expectant crowd, who knew
her for a martyr, as do I. Then at the last
I shut my eyes and stopped my ears,
and still I heard the wet smack
of the gunpowder, the snapping
as the fire rendered the bones.
To salve my soul I had this chapel built
but I hear them muttering in the walls
at night, in the narrow hours before dawn,
calling me Judas, Herod, Pilate all:
the stones weigh on me; are an old fool's guilt.

The library

(Anthony de Solempne, printer and merchant,
Albert Christiaensz & Joannes Paetz, printers and booksellers)

It is always the night hours
that take you back, slowly
as a page turning, to a book
which opens on acres of sea:

lettersnijder, textura say the waves,
and the dare-gale spinnaker
flyleafs from the top of the house
as the strakes of the room yaw

in a Norfolk breeze. It is always
the night hours, without the consolation
of the printed Word, without candles,
where superstition catches like serifs

on the breath. Garamond, roman, it is
always the night hours that come
with their strange litanies
to haul you back,

over the pamphleteering sea,
into the lands of rite and Antichrist,
where the works and outworks bloom
on cities in flower: what would you give

to be floated back there, drifting back
over the waters into the myth's eye,
to the depredations of Alba, to Breda
in the clutch of the beggar-years, and Leiden?

The great hall

But in that moment
when, at the height
of the dance

the drums and flutes
cease, and pour silence
over the floor

you will know:
these are strange times;
and the revellers

unmask themselves
to show bull's-heads,
basilisk-faces,

their grins and eyes
glowing and frenzied
in firelight

as they turn to you.
Pray the dancers
keep to their masque

in night corridors;
stranger,
keep to your hall -

lest you should find
the hunger
at the feast's centre

and the dark eyes
watching
from the wall.

The magazine
(riots in Norwich, 1648)

Freeze-frame, or woodcut.
A tongue of flame. A noise
like a great rushing of wind.
Glass in its midair poise.

What
there is
to be seen

is a boy,
turning his face
to the heat; a man

falling, his legs
smashed under him,
another floating beside him,

serene.

If I
could lead you
through the clouds

of burning gas,
past the heart
of the shockwave

into the moment,
into that fraction of a second
where the gunpowder

flashes,

you could take
that spark,
that ball of heat

and hold it

in the palm of your hand.

The garden
(Thomas Browne, 1605-1682)

What I remember are the fields
flooded with morning, and the birds:
waterways brilliant with coot-flocks,
hawks steady over hot lanes. Here

I remember them in studied walkways,
dust-mounted paths, my hours spent
in congelations, curdlings, turning
cow's milk with the rennet of a hare.

And turning in my chair I remember
the cold of the house in summer,
and the high tower of the church behind
where I once went about, hunting for tombs:

not yet, not yet. Remembering is all
that keeps from me the learned voices,
hushed as a page turning, talking Iliads
and scriptures among the racked tomes:

in whose keeping I leave my one day
past the point of Cromer, dancing
among September herring-shoals
as the shearwaters circled, higher

and higher – and still leaves me
crabbed in my chair from writing,
where the sun in passing leaves shade
in the house, and the quiet hours.

The vestry
(John Wesley, 1703-1791)

I went by and lo, he was gone. So I,
horse-sore, shivering, have seen the ungodly:
the strange shifting folk of byway thickets,
the packed sullen glances of the slums.

The old, coarse gospel beats its Sunday hours
steeple to steeple, flourishing like a green tree;
where I behold the upright, the wigged perfect
digress to Mancroft, by the same corruptible streets.

And the drab serious congregations
ready themselves for perfection with weeping;
having brought what comfort, dogged as I may,
I will return to that strange land, the roads,

the pace of a horse: leaving against hope
this gap in the air, this space. This kind of peace.

The drawing room
(Amelia Opie, 1769-1853)

Much as we peel back the details
in rococo paint and plaster to reveal
false ceilings, claustrophobic spaces
between floor and floor so

we strip out the quiet respectability
of Quakerhood, continental travels
and philanthropic gestures, down
to the raw fictions of a life,

the dash-it-all heady days
of wheelchair races and revolutions,
the brick-lined streets where the poor
radicals filed with you to the Octagon Chapel -

or further back, past the 'simple,
moral tales', the 'lines respectfully inscribed'
to the bloody bones
of Wollstonecraft and Bonaparte,

beyond the plasterboard facings
of the refined, impeccable wife
beyond even the giddy Jacobinism
and the guillotine's shadow

to the land where it is night
and the asylums are always full;
where a handful of toads, or beetles,
are a mother's promise to bring you

out of the coffin-spaces between walls
to the bright, cold rooms where
the small flames swing, in crystal,
and a window overlooks the gallows.

The stage door
(Edmund Kean, 1787-1833)

I am a villain. Yet I lie, I am not:
I am just an old man who plays
a villain. And not so old but fat,
and out of breath, with more grey hairs
than age is due. The drink, the clap,
the bawdy-houses and their pimps,
divorce and gambling: these are
my sins and I the laughing devil.
Yet I am none, however I
might prowl and pounce on backstage whores,
on Clarence, Anne, forever falling
on fakes and shadows, losing
the lines, the scene, the characters
for this unending paper snowstorm
which I must rail against, and go on
railing at even to the end.
I, who have taken bows and smiles
from the Gods take them now only
from the pit; I who have moved
the dark beyond the footlights
into love, or laughter now
no longer move myself, nor find
upon my bloated frame or gut
meat worth the moving. To be such:
venery, no more; was all I asked;
is all I have become, I empty
as the house is full. Behind me
scene-paint and brightness. In front:
thronged whispering space. I fear
I am not in my perfect mind.

The fireplace
(Harriet Martineau, 1802-1876;
James Martineau, 1805-1900)

1.
Dear Brother,
      fond   of our earlier
recollection I   I take exception to

how injurious   the reputation
          of this   dear friend
     how can you   ?

It hurts   you can have no conception
     how it pains me
that good,   , charitable,

whose efforts   seeking man's
     higher laws.
in thought   in whose

I remain

2.

H

       on intervening tracts

on time   I silently assume

             the living temple

the solemn eve

         which is not mine to take

which is not mine

          to repair.

if it were my chance

      it is not

I do not   of necessity,

      find the comprehension

        of these ideals, but

           bearing my own

humiliation and trust   this service,

     seeking   communion

endeavour   in this

     refit

       of neglected fires

The bedchamber
(Henry Crabb Robinson, diarist, 1775-1867)

As often on my couch I, spooling back
the years, unpick the babel of my life
I see it, clearly at times, at others
blurred as in a schoolboy's crib, the verb:

I labouring under the shadow of those
greater days, sending my letters home
from Austerlitz and Jena, in parlour-talk
with Lamb and Wordsworth, in continental tours;

but no mot juste, nothing to sum it up,
the Norfolk circuit and the London life,
the dust of law-books clotting in the mind
to make contentment foreign, and any bliss

far from verbatim in these books
where I am oblated from word to word.

The study

What intellectual manliness is left us,
according to him?
> *- J. H. Newman,*
> *Letter to the Duke of Norfolk*

By letter
to his grace the Duke:
can we be certain subjects
of temporal power? Citing
this, and other testaments
in my sermons

I find tedious. God,
how lovelier, how that much lovelier
to look upon than these dried
and bone-bare scrips; even in altar-glass,
in regular sacraments, than in this body
of narrowed words.

Yet I turn
to the narrowness of this room
as though a candle flickered
behind my hand, loading the long shadows
with landscapes, Dia, Senór,
that might be home.

In trust, and in
vocation how many of us
lodged? To care, and comfort,
though far from here, our charges
kept and in the keeping
of our church:

it sees us upright,
of manly intellect, until a time
when as elect, obedient
to, the light which comes
as through the crack of a doorway,
resumes.

The storm drain
(Floods in Norwich, 1912)

Slowly they will come back to you,
the wasted years. Slowly
through a quiet city
they will come

lapping their waters,
a valediction.

They too are the cargo:
of gaslights, prize bulls;

they will glide over
your empty wharves
curving the city
on its nightward sides;

the tanneries, the dyers'
yards on whose tides
stained, pleading with Yare

and Wensum they go under,
go. Slowly the salvage
drifts into hallways

on waters that will
unpick it, make it less
even than that: a litter

in morning's cobbled
monochrome.
A few drops
in the city's blood.

The auditorium
(Opening of The Regent cinema, 1922)

In which you will hear nothing
of the one man looking to bring
socialist policies to an enlightened
absolutism – admittedly by locking up

the rightful heir in Zenda,
hiring a sultry count (played here
by a gay Mexican) to exchange
lethal badinage with the faultless

double of the king – who will
in time warm to his role
as the asserter of homely
anglophone conservatism,

woo the crown princess, kill
the populist reform candidate,
expel bold Hentzau (over a waterfall)
and take himself off, ultimately,

quick-sharp. Because the film
is silent. Expect
non-stop Wurlitzer while
in a distant country (more real

than paranoid, representative
Ruritania) Lenin shoots his rivals,
founds his Republics, and history
steps over and inserts another reel:

enjoy it while it lasts, the duels,
the pasteboard palaces. Take heart
in its being still far away. The cinema
falls quiet at last. Outside the rain begins.

The cockpit
(Baedecker raids on Norwich, 27th and 29th April 1942)

The airframe roars. I,
Oberleutnant Hans Krickenberg
tune it like a violin
through the glissandi
of weave and rise, the stretto
of flak, the scherzoso
of dip and turbulence:

sometimes I hear myself
as on a gramophone
talking to the flight crew
about Mainz, or leave spent
chasing pretty girls in Lübeck
like some reminder
of the touring-car years,
of the pastoral sunshine between wars:

dreaming my dream of night-fighters
and search-beams. Sometimes
I see myself crawling
over the map of Europe,
punctured by specks of flame
of which this firelit steeple
is only one, and these streets
sparkle like stops in the divine
unending music of destruction.

The garret

Of which pedigrees
buttress-mounted
Mary-the-less genealogies,
wifi decorated, perpendicular
fan-vaulted obscurities
I am first and last:

most visible YouTube diffuser;
cross-media planner
of some note
in the burgh's fishwife tales,
less journeyman
than the barred wheel

which draws stone
like a fountain
into the anachronism,
the poised steel and glass concave.
I fritter images
like static

(neither the revelatory
belfry, counterpoising pinnacle,
nor Mussolini-inspired
town timepiece, neither
the culmination of the resolute
brick edifice, nor its adornment:

merely its checkpoint
with the clouds;
a gambit to bring crows
to winter windows;
a chance for broad glimpses
on the narrowest of things).

The grand civic space

Pax Romana in urbis sunt et cetera: we waffle
where we imagine senators once stood,
or romanised local thugs at any rate,
hawking their awful delicacies where we brew
our dreadful coffee, bake sub-par pizzas,
and look admiringly at our spare acreages
of glass, as though it made us newer, fresher,
more in tune with all the gothic oiks
who loiter on the steps. Ciabatta sir?
Perhaps a pasta salad? You'll notice we import
our wines from France, our mozzarella
straight from Poland and our staff
from Dagenham, where we are based.
It is so apt, so justly refreshing,
this shine spread over every surface,
the banisters of polished steel, the glass
wherever we could fit it, the floor tiles
which artfully recall the look of marble.
And the rest? Good honest English brick,
thank you – just look at anything
that's not the Eastern elevation. See that?
That's brick. And further up, featureless render
(well, when the builders came to tender
we skimped a little) and then the grandiose
and thoughtfully transparent roof which apes
the Circus Maximus, the Colosseum,
the basilica of Constantine – a triumph!
Bring on the gladiators led by Russell Crowe!
Bring on the lions and the Christians!
Let's have the mayor dressed as Caesar,
the councillors as Hercules and Apollo
while Janus smiles as patron on them all.
Laugh if you must. You'll find that by and large
we did far better than the fucking Castle Mall.

The museum after hours (2)

Consider this
history's last page
white

as the late frost
as the dust stirred
in night hours

the pen
set down
the recorder's footsteps

fading into the distance
it is not history
that

peers out on us
from a glass case
it is we who look

in
to call it the study
of the past

is to look
at dawn calling it
the dark of the moon

the dead make us
it is true
and we

in turn have made
of them
preface

to the purest
to the driven

snow

Notes

The foundations

The practice of looting building materials from older, disused structures (which has only abated in the last two hundred years) probably accounts for the disappearance of much of Roman Britain's architecture – in this case, the Roman town of Venta Icenorum – largely due to the demand for rubble infill between the dressed faces of mediaeval walls, and of course the eminently reusable nature of well-squared Roman masonry. The proverb refers to the village of Caistor St. Edmunds, built on the Roman site, which was eclipsed by Norwich's rise to prominence towards the start of the mediaeval period.

The layer of ash

Sweyn Forkbeard was among the last of the great warlords of the Viking age: his visit to Norwich, then a Saxon town of considerable size and the site of a royal mint, is recorded in the Anglo-Saxon chronicle as 'Her com Swegen mid his flotan to Norðwic, þa buruh eall geheregode forbærnde', which translates as 'This year came Sweyne with his fleet to Norwich, plundering and burning the whole town'. According to the C text of the chronicle (in which this entry appears), ealdorman Ulfcytel then led the men of East Anglia to an undecisive battle against Sweyn, after which both sides were so badly bloodied that they were forced to withdraw. Sweyn's fifteen years campaigning finally brought him the throne of England, but he did not live long enough to enjoy it. In this poem his triumph, played out in archaeological reconstruction, seems to have been somewhat cluttered by newer artefacts.

The undercroft

Many large mediaeval houses built before 1300, both in towns and in the countryside, were built upon a stone undercroft to protect them from the risks of fire (particularly problematic for town houses), from attack (in the case of fortified halls and early keeps) and from occasional flooding. This would then act as byre and household store, and, if necessary, accommodation for servants and dependants who could not be housed elsewhere. Most of the smells have their associations with Norwich, particularly the herring which, caught off the point of Cromer or Yarmouth and salted, were an important part of the mediaeval diet.

The vestibule

Herbert de Losinga (1054-1119), the Norman bishop responsible for removing the see of East Anglia from Thetford to Norwich, was in actual fact a man of real piety and talent. Although he almost certainly committed simony (which my poem hints at), and was punished accordingly, he appears to have repented, and rose to prominence in the reigns of William Rufus and Henry I.

The parlour

This poem is an attempt to quickly cast a murder mystery into verse: the few plausible accounts from the time state that, several days after being lured away from his mother's keeping by the bribes of a man claiming to be the archdeacon's cook with employment for him, the body of a boy named William was found in woodland, on Mousehold Heath with a wooden gag in his mouth, stabbed to death. Various unreliable testimonies put the boy in the house of Deus-adiuvet, one of the leading Jews of Norwich – an accusation that was quickly turned into a full-blown story of ritual murder (as distinct from blood libels), the earliest known accusation of its kind, and one which led to another of the anti-semitic pogroms that were so common in mediaeval Europe. Two years later the body of Deus-adiuvet was also found, almost certainly stabbed to death by the retainers of a knight who was in his debt and who may also have had some link to the circumstances surrounding William's murder.

Needless to say, a great deal of historical conjecture surrounds these disturbing events. Among the things the poem makes reference to are the angel, a mediaeval English coin (not introduced to England until much later, however), the more contemporary gold coins found in western Europe which were largely of Byzantine manufacture, William's later adoption as a saint by the canons of Norwich, and of course the role of Deus-adiuvet (like many other mediaeval Jews in Western Europe) as a moneylender.

The anchorhold

The anchorhold is an anchorite's cell; this one I have imagined occupied by Julian of Norwich, one of the more remarkable mystics of the high mediaeval church. This poem largely draws on her Revelations of Divine Love, perhaps the first book written by a woman in English.

The oubliette

This pantoum is based on a graffito found in the mediaeval dungeon of Norwich castle – the first stanza is a translation of it into modern English. Who Bartholomew was is unknown, but he was clearly possessed of some education (most of the other graffiti are crude figures or crosses) and spoke Norman French, the language of the nobility.

The oriel window

This poem, although it relates to the oriel window in the great
hall at Strangers', can easily be applied to the whole of England;
the covenant for the windows of the Beauchamp chapel is of little
relevance to Norwich except in its indication of the state of English
glassmaking for much of the mediaeval period: most glassware, and
most of the coloured glass used in the churches and cathedrals of
England was imported from the centres of production in Flanders
and northern France. But I find in the ties of the Beauchamp family to
the relentlessly expansionist Plantagenet throne – hence the anointed
land, the anointing of English kings after the French manner being a
Plantagenet innovation – something telling, and in its own way this
poem is a criticism aimed at the very heart of the Plantagenet vision of
England.

In the first two stanzas, it is worth noting that window-glass was
sold and measured by the square yard; and the donors (the people
responsible for financing the construction of a new window) would
often be depicted in their windows – the jumbling is a reference to
odd old pieces of mediaeval painted glass being leaded together in
later repairs and restorations.

The workshop

The arrival of communities of Dutch and Walloon weavers in the 16th
century, invited by the then mayor, Thomas Sotherton, was an attempt
to revive Norwich's own weaving industry, and by and large it
appears to have been a success. Turkey-work, something that Norwich
weavers were famous for, was an attempt to copy the Turkish carpets
that were then fashionable (and extortionately expensive) imports
from the Mediterranean; the spindle and the distaff are the simplest
of spinning tools; and like many trades at the time the weavers were
organised into studios wherein one or two masters would supervise a
larger team made up of journeymen and apprentices.

The private chapel

Elizabeth Cooper was one of the very few people burned for her faith in Nowich during the tumults of the reign of Queen Mary, and it seems (according to Foxe's great record of the time) that she was at least known to the same Thomas Sotherton who was at that time sheriff, and would later become mayor. Though the chapel is fictional, I have only mildly embellished Foxe's account of her death, which firmly states that Sotherton was compelled to arrest Cooper by the demands of another civic official, and his reluctance to do the same.

The library

Not only weavers crossed the channel from the Netherlands, however. The first printer in Norwich was the Dutch immigrant, Anthony de Solemne (actually more of an entrepreneur, since his main business in Norwich seemed to be trading in wine) who was almost certainly fleeing the Spanish armies as they attempted to subdue the United Provinces and return them to Roman Catholicism. It seems that he nevertheless had time to pack his printing equipment, and to bring with him two technical experts, Christiaensz and Paetz (of whom Paetz later resurfaces as a notable Dutch printer). It seems that their main efforts were expended in the production of prayer-books for the Dutch-speaking communities in England, and their press was only active for a few years. Lettersnijder, textura, garamond and roman are all typefaces used in Solemne's press; Leiden (whose horrific, protracted siege Solemne appears to have narrowly avoided) and Breda were both contested in the Dutch war of independence; 'beggar-years' is a reference to the Dutch fleet, who took a Spanish perjorative and made it their own, calling themselves sea-beggars (their timely intervention saved the starving defenders of Leiden); and the Duke of Alba was the chief Spanish general in the early phases of the war.

The magazine

This poem describes the disastrous end of a riot, probably of Royalist sympathies, which had initially broken out in support of Norwich's mayor. A large group of rioters, some of them armed, were cornered by soldiers in a building used to store gunpowder. When a stray spark accidentally ignited the 98 barrels of explosive powder, according to the most widely disseminated account as many as 200 were killed. The pamphlet describing these events, titled 'A true Relation of The late great Mutiny which was in the City and County of Norwich, April 24, 1648' which makes for an interesting read, can be found, among other places, at Early English Books Online.

The garden

Somewhat anachronistically, I picture Thomas Browne sitting in the garden at Strangers'. His copious notes on a far broader range of subjects than I could possibly convey in such a short poem make fascinating insight into the mind of a 17th-century intellectual, from his unfortunate efforts at 'translating' into Anglo-Saxon, to his innumerable small experiments, ponderings, and gleanings of information. Although most famous for his Pseudodoxia Epidemica, which debunks a number of widely-held errors on a range of subjects, he also believed in witches and was visited (and knighted) by Charles II on his visit to Norwich.

The vestry

John Wesley only visited Norwich a few times during his long career of itinerant preaching. He visited the newly-built Octagon Chapel, Thomas Ivory's architectural masterpiece, saying of it in his journal 'I was shewn Dr. Taylor's new meeting house, perhaps the most elegant one in all Europe. The inside is finished in the highest taste and is as clean as any nobleman's saloon. The communion table is fine mahogany; the very latches of the pew doors are polished brass. How can it be that the old coarse gospel should find admission here?' This poem draws heavily on his funeral address for John Fletcher, which in turn took as its reading the 37th Psalm, lines from which can be easily recognised in my version. Perfection is, in this poem, meant in its religious sense of the apogee of human holiness – controversies over which dogged Wesley's career from time to time. And of course Mancroft is the parish church of St. Peter Mancroft, one of the richest and most conservative parishes in the city and thus in some opposition to Wesley's unitarianism.

The drawing room

Amelia Opie, the 18th - and 19th -century writer was, as so many of the people of her generation, an admirer of the French revolution, at least initially. Having been brought up in a relatively liberal dissenting family – the Opies were among the first rank of dissenting families of Norwich - her conversion to Quakerism was probably not entirely congenial to her, and the incidents I hint at, the wheelchair races, and her mother confronting her with creatures she feared such as toads and beetles (to eradicate her irrational temperament) did indeed take place. The quotations 'simple, moral tales' and 'lines respectfully inscribed' are indeed taken from her writings, the latter of which being part of the title of one of her poems. I have set this poem in the rococo drawing room of Strangers' Hall, which does indeed have a false ceiling, inserted when the room was created at the museum's inception.

The stage door

The great actor, Edmund Kean, did indeed come to Norwich on one of his several farewell tours. His addictions to women, gambling and drink were notorious, and his attendant disregard for his own health shortened both his life and his acting career, the latter of which was only extended by the pressures of his continual proximity to bankruptcy. His first great role was that of Richard III (a critic did indeed describe him as a 'laughing devil'), and when he came to Norwich he was cast in his last significant role, that of Shakespeare's Lear, so the poem begins and ends with quotes from each of these plays.

The fireplace

Harriet and James Martineau, the estranged but brilliant brother
and sister from Norwich, remind me somewhat of the excellent
17th-century dragons in the moulding on either side of the fireplaces
of Strangers Hall. Harriet Martineau was a prolific correspondent,
but none of her letters to her brother from the period of their
estrangement survive: as she writes to Henry Crabb Robinson (who
also figures in this book) 'my letters are... a flowing out of the moment
to you and the fire.' Harriet, convinced of the cure by mesmerism
of an ovarian cyst which very nearly killed her, turned away from
the unitarianism of her upbringing, making a complete break in her
relationship with her brother James, who had become one of the
foremost unitarian ministers of the day.

Harriet's poem (the first one) is based on her letters and
autobiography; James' is based on one of his most remarkable
sermons, from a few years before the break, usually called The Watch-
Night Lamps. Although Harriet is generally considered to have had
the last word through her autobiography, I have here allowed James
to conclude.

The bedchamber

Henry Crabb Robinson is more famous by association than deed: his
diaries offer considerable insight into the literary and social circles
of Wordsworth and Coleridge, among others, and he appears in
Wordsworth's poem *The Excursion*. He had some success as a lawyer
on the Norwich circuit, and was the Times' correspondent during the
years of Bonaparte's most striking successes but as an individual he
always seems, even in his own account of his life, somewhat marginal
– a sentiment that I have tried to convey here.

The study

Immediately prior to its restoration as a museum, Strangers' Hall was used as lodgings for some of the city's Catholic clergy, and this poem is consequently set in the rambling attics and upper rooms of Strangers'. John Henry Newman was probably the leading Catholic voice of his day in the United Kingdom, and his open letter to the Duke of Norfolk, the country's leading Catholic layman, seemed like a good point of contact between Norwich (where the Dukes built the cathedral of John the Baptist) and the wider world of the Catholic church. It is entirely possible that the epithet 'strangers' comes from this period, especially in view of the latent anti-catholicism of the English laity.

The storm drain

In many respects the Wensum-Yare has been overlooked in these poems, important as it was for downriver trade to Yarmouth and the sea. The dyers' workshops and tanneries, which once formed a large part of Norwich's industry, were always in districts next to the river to allow water to be drawn and waste to be speedily removed, though they had all but disappeared by the time of the flood. The prize bulls are a reference to Norwich's busy livestock market which, until its removal in the 1970s, was a prominent feature of the city centre.

The auditorium

The title is ironic: the 1922 *Prisoner of Zenda* was a silent film, in which Rupert of Hentzau was indeed played by the gay Mexican actor, Ramon Novarro. It was, and is, a piece of pure escapism which implicitly reinforces a kind of anglophone conservatism that stands in uneasy relation to the disturbing political climate of the time. The Regent Cinema stood on Prince of Wales Rd. where its building is still standing.

The cockpit

The Luftwaffe officer of this piece is fictional; the air raid is certainly not. The Baedecker raids, launched in retaliation to the destruction of most of the pretty Hanseatic League city of Lübeck by Allied incendiary bombs, were intended to destroy monuments of English culture, an objective in which they largely failed: Norwich lost only a few parish churches in the raid. By far the worst damage was done to ordinary housing, while the cathedral, the castle, and most of its other historic buildings escaped largely undamaged.

The garret

Many terms here are modern and require little explanation, but some are not, and do: Mary the Less was the church made over for the Dutch and Walloon immigrants of the 16th century, parish churches in general being a great source of genealogical information; the perpendicular and decorated styles were periods in English religious architecture, the fan-vault being a feature of the latter; and lastly the 'barred wheel' is in fact a treadmill, usually worked by draught animals and used by mediaeval builders to raise masonry to the height of their current phase of construction.

The grand civic space

This skit on the proliferation of Italian-themed eateries, and on the modern architect's obsession with steel, glass and concrete, makes some reference to Roman tradition: the opening is the garbled dog-Latin of the sort used to justify sub-Roman despots throughout Europe. Janus, the two-faced god of Roman tradition did indeed supervise the door of the senate house; and it was customary, particularly in the more Hellenised parts of the empire, for the statues of emperors to take on the likenesses of particularly propitious gods.

Also from Gatehouse Press...

Shuck, Hick, Tiffey!

George Szirtes

Three libretti based on Norfolk myths and folktales from
internationally renowned poet and translator George Szirtes. Written
for children and performed at Wymondham, this hardback edition
includes some of the original score writen by Ken Crandell.

'George Szirtes, one of our most eminent poets, is a sophisticated
and resourceful explorer of the 'language forest'; he forges personal
experience and profound analytical observation of the world into
works of compelling and original power.' — *Penelope Shuttle*

ISBN: 978 0 9554770 8 9

As The Crow Flies

Jo Kjaer

Winner of the 2008 Café Writers Norfolk Poetry Commission 'As The Crow Flies' represents author Jo Kjaer's first poetry collection, winning the inaugural Café Writers Norfolk Poetry Commission. She gained a first in the Advanced Poetry Diploma at the University of East Anglia in 2007, and teaches Creative Writing for the National Extension College.

The Café Writers Norfolk Commission is a new annual poetry competition, open to recent graduates from a creative writing based course at Norwich School of Art and Design and the UEA, to support emerging literary talent and build a body of poetry which responds to the county in some way.

"It is a fascinating idea to write poems with OS map references attached: somewhere between poem-biography and conceptual art, it constitutes a new kind of marriage between the lyrical poem and the notion of provenance. Where precisely in Stoke Poges churchyard was Gray sitting? Which view of Tintern Abbey did Wordsworth have in mind when visiting the Wye Valley? Jo Kjaer's collection is intimately related to points in the Norfolk landscape. The poems are subtle points of clarity, riffs arising from specific settings, brief love letters to place, powerfully held together by the overall project which is the inscription of experience on place." — *George Szirtes*

ISBN: 978 0 9554770 6 5

Undercurrents

Edited by Benjamin Scott

A Venusian child contemplates a future returning to place long left behind…
A cantankerous elderly lady engages in a battle of wits with a youthful adversary…
A pair of Lancastrian weavers work their sales pitch – in Biblical Judea…
'Undercurrents', from students of Norfolk Adult Education's Advanced Creative Writing course is a diverse collection of short stories; a series of worlds that burst into being, flicker into life then disappear, within the space of a few pages. This deep, compelling and resonant anthology offers the reader fleeting - yet complete - glimpses into these worlds, where journeys flow through time, place and perspective, and move through pervading moods of fear and tension, into innocence and hopefulness.

ISBN: 978 0 9554770 5 8

About Gatehouse Press

Gatehouse Press is a publishing house based in Norwich. Created in 2006, its aim is to support new writers, primarily through publishing poetry and short story.

Our talented team works hard to create and maintain a level of quality that remains unrivalled. Our books get great feedback and are reviewed by some of Norfolk's top writers.

For more information, and to order our books, please visit our website:

www.gatehousepress.com